This book belongs to:

_____

# ANGEL MOON
## 2022

Angel Moon 2022
Journal

Copyright © 2021 by Crystal Sky
www.psychic-emails.com

Mystic Cat

The information accessible from this book is for informational purposes only. No statement within is a promise of benefits. There is no guarantee of any results.

Images are under license from Shutterstock, Dreamstime, or Deposit-photos.

# 2022

## JANUARY
| M | T | W | T | F | S | S |
|---|---|---|---|---|---|---|
|   |   |   |   |   | 1 | 2 |
| 3 | 4 | 5 | 6 | 7 | 8 | 9 |
| 10 | 11 | 12 | 13 | 14 | 15 | 16 |
| 17 | 18 | 19 | 20 | 21 | 22 | 23 |
| 24 | 25 | 26 | 27 | 28 | 29 | 30 |
| 31 |   |   |   |   |   |   |

## FEBRUARY
| M | T | W | T | F | S | S |
|---|---|---|---|---|---|---|
|   | 1 | 2 | 3 | 4 | 5 | 6 |
| 9 | 10 | 11 | 12 | 11 | 12 | 13 |
| 14 | 15 | 16 | 17 | 18 | 19 | 20 |
| 21 | 22 | 23 | 24 | 25 | 26 | 27 |
| 28 |   |   |   |   |   |   |

## MARCH
| M | T | W | T | F | S | S |
|---|---|---|---|---|---|---|
|   | 1 | 2 | 3 | 4 | 4 | 6 |
| 7 | 8 | 9 | 10 | 11 | 12 | 13 |
| 14 | 15 | 16 | 17 | 18 | 19 | 20 |
| 21 | 22 | 23 | 24 | 25 | 26 | 27 |
| 28 | 29 | 30 | 31 |   |   |   |

## APRIL
| M | T | W | T | F | S | S |
|---|---|---|---|---|---|---|
|   |   |   |   | 1 | 2 | 3 |
| 4 | 5 | 6 | 7 | 8 | 9 | 10 |
| 11 | 12 | 13 | 14 | 15 | 16 | 17 |
| 18 | 19 | 20 | 21 | 22 | 23 | 24 |
| 25 | 26 | 27 | 28 | 29 | 30 |   |

## MAY
| M | T | W | T | F | S | S |
|---|---|---|---|---|---|---|
|   |   |   |   |   |   | 1 |
| 2 | 3 | 4 | 5 | 6 | 7 | 8 |
| 9 | 10 | 11 | 12 | 13 | 14 | 15 |
| 16 | 17 | 18 | 19 | 20 | 21 | 22 |
| 23 | 24 | 25 | 26 | 27 | 28 | 29 |
| 30 | 31 |   |   |   |   |   |

## JUNE
| M | T | W | T | F | S | S |
|---|---|---|---|---|---|---|
|   |   | 1 | 2 | 3 | 4 | 5 |
| 6 | 7 | 8 | 9 | 10 | 11 | 12 |
| 13 | 14 | 15 | 16 | 17 | 18 | 19 |
| 20 | 21 | 22 | 23 | 24 | 25 | 26 |
| 27 | 28 | 29 | 30 |   |   |   |

## JULY
| M | T | W | T | F | S | S |
|---|---|---|---|---|---|---|
|   |   |   |   | 1 | 2 | 3 |
| 4 | 5 | 6 | 7 | 8 | 9 | 10 |
| 11 | 12 | 13 | 14 | 15 | 16 | 17 |
| 18 | 19 | 20 | 21 | 22 | 23 | 24 |
| 25 | 26 | 27 | 28 | 29 | 30 | 31 |

## AUGUST
| M | T | W | T | F | S | S |
|---|---|---|---|---|---|---|
| 1 | 2 | 3 | 4 | 5 | 6 | 7 |
| 8 | 9 | 10 | 11 | 12 | 13 | 14 |
| 15 | 16 | 17 | 18 | 19 | 20 | 21 |
| 22 | 23 | 24 | 25 | 26 | 27 | 28 |
| 29 | 30 | 31 |   |   |   |   |

## SEPTEMBER
| M | T | W | T | F | S | S |
|---|---|---|---|---|---|---|
|   |   |   | 1 | 2 | 3 | 4 |
| 5 | 6 | 7 | 8 | 9 | 10 | 11 |
| 12 | 13 | 14 | 15 | 16 | 17 | 18 |
| 19 | 20 | 21 | 22 | 23 | 24 | 25 |
| 26 | 27 | 28 | 29 | 30 |   |   |

## OCTOBER
| M | T | W | T | F | S | S |
|---|---|---|---|---|---|---|
|   |   |   |   |   | 1 | 2 |
| 3 | 4 | 5 | 6 | 7 | 8 | 9 |
| 10 | 11 | 12 | 13 | 14 | 15 | 16 |
| 17 | 18 | 19 | 20 | 21 | 22 | 23 |
| 24 | 25 | 26 | 27 | 28 | 29 | 30 |
| 31 |   |   |   |   |   |   |

## NOVEMBER
| M | T | W | T | F | S | S |
|---|---|---|---|---|---|---|
|   | 1 | 2 | 3 | 4 | 5 | 6 |
| 7 | 8 | 9 | 10 | 11 | 12 | 13 |
| 14 | 15 | 16 | 17 | 18 | 19 | 20 |
| 21 | 22 | 23 | 24 | 25 | 26 | 27 |
| 28 | 29 | 30 |   |   |   |   |

## DECEMBER
| M | T | W | T | F | S | S |
|---|---|---|---|---|---|---|
|   |   |   | 1 | 2 | 3 | 4 |
| 5 | 6 | 7 | 8 | 9 | 10 | 11 |
| 12 | 13 | 14 | 15 | 16 | 17 | 18 |
| 19 | 20 | 21 | 22 | 23 | 24 | 25 |
| 26 | 27 | 28 | 29 | 30 | 31 |   |

# 2023

## JANUARY

| M | T | W | T | F | S | S |
|---|---|---|---|---|---|---|
|   |   |   |   |   |   | 1 |
| 2 | 3 | 4 | 5 | 6 | 7 | 8 |
| 9 | 10 | 11 | 12 | 13 | 14 | 15 |
| 16 | 17 | 18 | 19 | 20 | 21 | 22 |
| 23 | 24 | 25 | 26 | 27 | 28 | 29 |
| 30 | 31 |   |   |   |   |   |

## FEBRUARY

| M | T | W | T | F | S | S |
|---|---|---|---|---|---|---|
|   |   | 1 | 2 | 3 | 4 | 5 |
| 6 | 7 | 8 | 9 | 10 | 11 | 12 |
| 13 | 14 | 15 | 16 | 17 | 18 | 19 |
| 20 | 21 | 22 | 23 | 24 | 25 | 26 |
| 27 | 28 |   |   |   |   |   |

## MARCH

| M | T | W | T | F | S | S |
|---|---|---|---|---|---|---|
|   |   | 1 | 2 | 3 | 4 | 5 |
| 6 | 7 | 8 | 9 | 10 | 11 | 12 |
| 13 | 14 | 15 | 16 | 17 | 18 | 19 |
| 20 | 21 | 22 | 23 | 24 | 25 | 26 |
| 27 | 28 | 29 | 30 | 31 |   |   |

## APRIL

| M | T | W | T | F | S | S |
|---|---|---|---|---|---|---|
|   |   |   |   |   | 1 | 2 |
| 3 | 4 | 5 | 6 | 7 | 8 | 9 |
| 10 | 11 | 12 | 13 | 14 | 15 | 16 |
| 17 | 18 | 19 | 20 | 21 | 22 | 23 |
| 24 | 25 | 26 | 27 | 28 | 29 | 30 |

## MAY

| M | T | W | T | F | S | S |
|---|---|---|---|---|---|---|
| 1 | 2 | 3 | 4 | 5 | 6 | 7 |
| 8 | 9 | 10 | 11 | 12 | 13 | 14 |
| 15 | 16 | 17 | 18 | 19 | 20 | 21 |
| 22 | 23 | 24 | 25 | 26 | 27 | 28 |
| 29 | 30 | 31 |   |   |   |   |

## JUNE

| M | T | W | T | F | S | S |
|---|---|---|---|---|---|---|
|   |   |   | 1 | 2 | 3 | 4 |
| 5 | 6 | 7 | 8 | 9 | 10 | 11 |
| 12 | 13 | 14 | 15 | 16 | 17 | 18 |
| 19 | 20 | 21 | 22 | 23 | 24 | 25 |
| 26 | 27 | 28 | 29 | 30 |   |   |

## JULY

| M | T | W | T | F | S | S |
|---|---|---|---|---|---|---|
|   |   |   |   |   | 1 | 2 |
| 3 | 4 | 5 | 6 | 7 | 8 | 9 |
| 10 | 11 | 12 | 13 | 14 | 15 | 16 |
| 17 | 18 | 19 | 20 | 21 | 22 | 23 |
| 24 | 25 | 26 | 27 | 28 | 29 | 30 |
| 31 |   |   |   |   |   |   |

## AUGUST

| M | T | W | T | F | S | S |
|---|---|---|---|---|---|---|
|   | 1 | 2 | 3 | 4 | 5 | 6 |
| 7 | 8 | 9 | 10 | 11 | 12 | 13 |
| 14 | 15 | 16 | 17 | 18 | 19 | 20 |
| 21 | 22 | 23 | 24 | 25 | 26 | 27 |
| 28 | 29 | 30 | 31 |   |   |   |

## SEPTEMBER

| M | T | W | T | F | S | S |
|---|---|---|---|---|---|---|
|   |   |   |   | 1 | 2 | 3 |
| 4 | 5 | 6 | 7 | 8 | 9 | 10 |
| 11 | 12 | 13 | 14 | 15 | 16 | 17 |
| 18 | 19 | 20 | 21 | 22 | 23 | 24 |
| 25 | 26 | 27 | 28 | 29 | 30 |   |

## OCTOBER

| M | T | W | T | F | S | S |
|---|---|---|---|---|---|---|
|   |   |   |   |   |   | 1 |
| 2 | 3 | 4 | 5 | 6 | 7 | 8 |
| 9 | 10 | 11 | 12 | 13 | 14 | 15 |
| 16 | 17 | 18 | 19 | 20 | 21 | 22 |
| 23 | 24 | 25 | 26 | 27 | 28 | 29 |
| 30 | 31 |   |   |   |   |   |

## NOVEMBER

| M | T | W | T | F | S | S |
|---|---|---|---|---|---|---|
|   |   | 1 | 2 | 3 | 4 | 5 |
| 6 | 7 | 8 | 9 | 10 | 11 | 12 |
| 13 | 14 | 15 | 16 | 17 | 18 | 19 |
| 20 | 21 | 22 | 23 | 24 | 25 | 26 |
| 27 | 28 | 29 | 30 |   |   |   |

## DECEMBER

| M | T | W | T | F | S | S |
|---|---|---|---|---|---|---|
|   |   |   |   | 1 | 2 | 3 |
| 4 | 5 | 6 | 7 | 8 | 9 | 10 |
| 11 | 12 | 13 | 14 | 15 | 16 | 17 |
| 18 | 19 | 20 | 21 | 22 | 23 | 24 |
| 25 | 26 | 27 | 28 | 29 | 30 | 31 |

## 2022 Full Moons

Wolf Moon: January 17th, 23:48.

Snow Moon: February 16th, 16:57

Worm Moon March 18th, 07:17

Pink Moon: April 16th, 18:54

Flower Moon: May 16th, 04:13

Strawberry Moon: June 14th, 11:51

Buck Moon: July 13th, 18:37

Sturgeon Moon: August 12th, 01:35

Corn, Harvest Moon: September 10th, 09:59

Hunters Moon: October 9th, 20:54

Beaver Moon: November 8th, 11:01

Cold Moon: December 8th, 04:07

## 2022 At A Glance

### Eclipses

Partial Solar – April 30th

Total Lunar – May 16th

Partial Solar – October 25th

Total Lunar -November 8th

### Equinoxes and Solstices

Spring - March 20th

Summer - June 21st

Fall – September 23rd

Winter – December 21st

### Mercury Retrogrades

January 14th, Aquarius - February 4th Capricorn

May 10th, Gemini - June 3rd, Taurus

September 10th, Libra - October 2nd Virgo

December 29th, Capricorn - January 1st, 2023, Capricorn

## The Moon Phases

- New Moon (Dark Moon)

- Waxing Crescent Moon

- First Quarter Moon

- Waxing Gibbous Moon

- Full Moon

- Waning Gibbous (Disseminating) Moon

- Third (Last/Reconciling) Quarter Moon

- Waning Crescent (Balsamic) Moon

## ◑ New Moon (Dark Moon)

The New Moon reveals what hides beyond the realm of everyday circumstances. It creates space to focus on contemplation and the gathering of wisdom. It is the beginning of the moon cycles. It is a time for plotting your course and planning for the future. It does let you unearth new possibilities when you tap into the wisdom of what is flying under the radar. You can embrace positivity, change, and adaptability. Harness the New Moon's power to set the stage for developing your trailblazing ideas. It is a Moon phase for hatching plans for nurturing ideas. Creativity is quickening; thoughts are flexible and innovative. Epiphanies are prevalent during this time.

## ◑ Waxing Crescent Moon

It is the Moon's first step forward on her journey towards fullness. Change is in the air, it can feel challenging to see the path ahead, yet something is tempting you forward. Excitement and inspiration are in the air. It epitomizes a willingness to be open to change and grow your world. This Moon often brings surprises, good news, seed money, and secret information. This Moon brings opportunities that are a catalyst for change. It tempts the debut of wild ideas and goals. It catapults you towards growth and often brings a breakthrough that sweeps in and demands your attention. Changes in the air, inspiration weaves the threads of manifestation around your awareness.

## First Quarter Moon

The First Quarter Moon is when exactly half of the Moon is shining. It signifies that action is ready to be taken. You face a crossroads; decisive action clears the path. You cut through indecisiveness and make your way forward. There is a sense of something growing during this phase. Your creativity nourishes the seeds you planted. As you reflect on this journey, you draw equilibrium and balance the First Quarter Moon's energy before tipping the scales in your favor. You feel a sense of accomplishment of having made progress on your journey, yet, there is still a long way to go. Pause, take time to contemplate the path ahead, and begin to nurture your sense of perseverance and grit as things have a ways to go.

## Waxing Gibbous Moon

Your plans are growing; the devil is in the detail; a meticulous approach lets you achieve the highest result. You may find a boost arrives and gives a shot of can-do energy. It connects you with new information about the path ahead. The Moon is growing, as is your creativity, inspiration, and focus. It is also a time of essential adjustments, streamlining, evaluating goals, and plotting your course towards the final destination. Success is within reach; a final push will get you through. The wind is beneath your wings, a conclusion within reach, and you have the tools at your disposal to achieve your vision.

## ◉ Full Moon

The Full Moon is when you often reach a successful conclusion. It does bring a bounty that adds to your harvest. Something unexpected often unfolds that transforms your experience. It catches you by surprise, a breath of fresh air; it is a magical time that lets you appreciate what your work has achieved. It is time for communication and sharing thoughts and ideas. It often brings a revelation eliminating new information. The path clears, and you release doubt, anxiety, and tension. It is a therapeutic and healing time that lets you release old energy positively and supportively.

## ◉ Waning Gibbous (Disseminating) Moon

The Waning gibbous Moon is perfect for release; it allows you to cut away from areas that hold back true potential. You may feel drained as you have worked hard, journeyed long, and are now creating space to return and complete the cycle. It does see tools arrive to support and nourish your spirit. Creating space to channel your energy effectively and cutting away outworn regions creates an environment that lets your ideas and efforts bloom. It is a healing time, a time of acceptance that things move forward towards completing a cycle. This the casting off the outworn, the debris that accumulates over the lunar month is a vital cleansing that clears space and resolves complex emotions that may cling to your energy if not addressed.

## Third (Last/Reconciling) Quarter Moon

This Moon is about stabilizing your foundations. There is uncertainty, shifting sands; as change surrounds your life, take time to be mindful of drawing balance into your world. It is the perfect time to reconnect with simple past times and hobbies. Securing and tethering your energy does build a stable foundation from which to grow your world. It is time to take stock and balance areas of your life. Consolidating your power, nurturing your inner child lets you embrace a chapter to focus on the areas that bring you joy. It is not time to advance or acquire new goals. It's a restful phase that speaks of simple pastimes that nurture your spirit.

## Waning Crescent (Balsamic) Moon

The Waning Crescent Moon completes the cycle; it is the Moon that finishes the set. It lets you tie up loose ends, finish the finer details, and essentially creates space for new inspiration to flow into your world once the cycle begins again. The word balsamic speaks of healing and attending to areas that feel raw or sensitive. It is a mystical phase that reconnects you to the cycle of life. As the Moon dies away, you can move away from areas that feel best left behind. A focus on healing, meditation, self-care, and nurturing one's spirit is essential during this Moon phase.

## The Archangels

Archangels are always around you; sometimes, you need one particular Angel more than another. Depending on your current life circumstances, one or more angels will be walking the journey carefully with you. Archangels come into our lives with their love, understanding, and compassion. They work for the highest spirit and seek to protect and empower you to be the best version of yourself. They encourage and support us. Archangels come to us with love, acceptance, understanding, and deep compassion.

Archangels are trusted allies in the spirit world who protect and offer guidance. They can give you the ideas needed to choose wisely for your situation. When you feel downhearted, they nurture your spirit and send bright blessings into your world. Their love epitomizes grace, generosity, and understanding. They broaden your perception, allowing you to detach from issues and see your world in a new light. They teach you new tricks and strengthen your reserves of grit and resilience. Before long, you begin to see that the obstacle is, in fact, the way forward towards newfound growth and prosperity. You can call on your archangels whenever you need guidance and support; they send love and bring the knowledge that you never walk alone. Here are the 15 main known Archangels and their role in your life.

## Archangel Ariel ~ Lioness of God

Ariel is the guardian and healer of animals. Call upon her when you seek to communicate with animals that have passed over or are in your life. Ariel also rules over the natural world, and when in nature, she is nearby. She is warm and hospitable with a caring, sensitive environment. Her energy is powerful yet gentle. She inspires natural growth and encourages people to live to their full potential. Her role is to make you aware of the vital role that animals can have in your life. They provide a close network of support, which is essential to nurture the gifts of empathy and compassion. Animals are a blessing and bring luck and fortune into our lives when treated with love and compassion. Kindness to all animals is associated with healthful benefits that draw abundance into your life.

Ariel seeks to elevate your life and connect you with a divine aspect that harmonizes your spirit. It releases outworn energy, healing the past, and offers a therapeutic flow of new energy that calms and soothes. It brings a journey that is both intense and fascinating. It provides the right conditions to dig deep and reveal an aspect within that seeks discovery. Slowing down the pace lets you integrate change and journey onward.

## Archangel Azrael ~ Whom God helps

Azrael is the Angel of Death. Do not be scared of this title as, like the tarot card, he offers you transformation during difficult times. He provides comfort for families and friends who are grieving the loss of a loved one. He guides them to the light to reconnect with their loved ones in the spirit world for those who passed. He offers compassion and wisdom. His energy is comforting, patient, and understanding. His softly spoken words say that your loved ones are gifts from heaven, which return to the source when they finish earthly work. Always appreciate the moments you are blessed to spend with them. The mere knowledge that these are borrowed gifts from heaven enables you to enjoy the blessings they bring to your life. After losing a loved one, call on his support for healing.

## Archangel Chamuel ~ He who sees God

Chamuel embodies generosity, love, and compassion. He makes us more aware of the love and compassion in ourselves. Understanding the grace we hold within our spirit also allows us to attract more positivity into our environment. He is also known for raising intuition and spiritual vibrations and tuning into channeled messages from the divine and higher spirits. His energy is loving, tender, and sympathetic. Chamuel is a good listener with a generous heart. Chamuel helps balance interpersonal bonds and draws the right people into your journey. You can call upon him to protect your world. It creates barriers from the nefarious individuals who are not on a higher level of evolution and do not resonate with genuine kindness and compassion to others. It is his work to help you find the right people for your journey in this world. He offers protection from those who would harm.

**Archangel Gabriel** ~ Strength of God

Gabriel heightens creativity, giving you the ability to develop your inherent gifts of writing, art, music, verbal expression, and emotional expression. Gabriel is graceful, elegant, and uplifting. Her words are positive, encouraging, and inspiring. She communicates her wisdom with the intent of creating positive change and growth. You can call upon Gabriel when you need help understanding, accepting, and passing messages from the spiritual realm.

Gabrielle offers strength, guidance, and acceptance. She resonates with the announcement that taking stock of your situation is helpful. Accept what cannot be changed but continue to look for solutions to create the shift you would like to see. So much is within your grasp if you allow your vision to take flight. Your ideas have wings; they seek manifestation in your life.

## Archangel Haniel ~ Grace of God

Haniel brings gifts of heightened intuition, receptivity, and self-awareness. Haniel guides those who seek to develop their psychic abilities, spiritual talents, and even healing arts. Her energy is healing, soothing, and patient. She helps restore equilibrium and is a profoundly caring Angel. She offers relaxation with her gifts of uplifting your spirit and rejuvenates your soul. She is colorful, nurturing, and conscientious. She speaks with thoughtfulness and understanding. Call on her for words of wisdom, grace, and knowledge. Suppose you are interested in the esoteric arts. In that case, she is your go-to Angel if you want to increase your intuitive and psychic abilities.

**Archangel Jeremiel ~** Mercy of God

Jeremiel is the Angel of faith and hope. He is one of the main Archangels who help people cross over to the spiritual realm. He guides souls to review their life on earth and helps people learn from their mistakes. He also brings prophetic dreams and visions. Jeremiel resonates with the energy of compassion and mercy. He enables you to gain insight into areas that feel murky. He illuminates a path forward, which helps dissipate the fog, allowing you to gain clarity. Call on him. Suppose you seek to understand a situation better. In that case, his wisdom shines an intense beam forward, allowing you to discover the truth.

**Archangel Jophiel ~** Beauty of God

Jophiel helps us when we feel lost. She lets us become aware of the grace and beauty of our souls. She doesn't focus on physical attractiveness. She teaches people to search deep within themselves and gain the confidence needed to express themselves openly from the heart. She helps us see the beauty in others and our environment to appreciate and be grateful for what we have. Jophiel is gracious, inviting, and elegant; she speaks softly and in gentle tones. She reminds people who they are inside and what they can become if they set the bar higher for themselves and those around them.

**Archangel Metatron** ~ Highest of Angels (twin)

Angel Metatron is a twin of Sandalphon; they were both once human but ascended as Angels. He is connected to the Book of Life and takes meticulous records of all that happens on earth. He helps those who need motivation, discipline, and organization. He can help those starting a new endeavor or project and who need help with time management or organization. His energy connects to the essence of being human. Because he was once human, he understands essential human traits and weaknesses. Archangel Metatron offers down-to-earth advice; he is direct and analytical. He can assist you with practical matters.

**Archangel Michael** ~ One who is like God

Archangel Michael is one of the best-known Archangels. Featured in a blockbuster movie, Michael is often called upon by those currently eath bound. Michael is accommodating when it comes to spiritual protection and cleansing. He is everyone's favorite protector and guardian. Michael possesses strength and courage. Archangel, Michael helps connect you with your destiny and actual life purposes. He can clear out any negative energies which are around your life. Archangel Michael is a big personality who has an enormous presence in your life. His keen sense of purpose enables you to move out of your comfort zone, release doubt, dispel fear, and move beyond your limitations. He is ethical, righteous, and one who has firmly held ideals. He is selfless, disciplined, and genuinely desires to improve your life by releasing all barriers that keep your potential held back.

Michael says that focusing on the building blocks of your life lets you achieve impressive results. Feel free to explore side journeys that speak to your soul as these little worn tracks hold meaning and grace for your life. It does have you feeling ready to develop plans for the future. Taking time to pause and reflect on the changes that swirl around your life draws balance.

## Archangel Raguel ~ The friend of God

Archangel Raguel is the Angel of Justice; Raguel resonates with truth and honesty. He presides over our lives as a mediator, helping us in challenging situations. He restores balance and equilibrium; he draws peace and well-being into our environment. He can also help resolve issues that cause stress or anxiety. His energy embodies logic and unbiasedness. Archangel Raguel is practical and offers realistic and achievable solutions. Justice is his passion; he is passionate and dedicated in his quest to correct the world's wrongs. He is righteous, an Angel who is tenacious with a sturdy inner shield.

**Archangel Raphael ~ God heals**

Raphael draws inner and outer healing (mental, emotional, physical, spiritual). It improves our lives by promoting better health and spirituality. Archangel Raphael is a genuinely caring person who was profoundly ethical. His big heart knows no boundaries. Raphael comforts and heals past and present emotional wounds. Raphael helps you to improve emotionally, mentally, even physically. Archangel Raphael helps release toxic energy, which drains your inner reserves. He is a magnetic and warmhearted Angel whose purpose is to improve your emotional terrain. Raphael sees your life as a journey of self-discovery. Raphael wants to see you inspired and ready to embark on new adventures. He wisely knows that creating a stable foundation is the first step in achieving your highest result.

Archangel Raphael walks beside you and says you are someone with enormous courage and emotional strength. Discovering your life purpose draws a therapeutic aspect into your surroundings as you do best when on a mission. He says that having a worthy cause to dedicate your energy towards, heart and soul brings light into your life.

## Archangel Raziel ~ Secrets of God

Archangel Raziel heightens our faith and belief in the divine and the spiritual world. He possesses a profound understanding of life; he encourages us to strengthen our bonds to the spiritual realm and seek help and guidance from the divine and the Archangels' wisdom. Raziel is mature and wise. Raziel is direct, intelligent, and insightful. Raziel helps you to restore faith, trust, and confidence. Having a strong sense of belief in the divine is positively associated with longevity. It supports your well-being in many ways. Raziel is pleased to be there to keep your personal growth.

Raziel is an angel who connects you to a path of higher purpose and divinity. This Angel surrounds your life with creative and visionary energy. He helps you get back into emotional equilibrium during difficult times. This Angel attracts synchronicity into your life to provide clues that guide you towards a divine aspect. Connecting with this Archangel is tremendously beneficial for your life.

**Archangel Sandalphon** ~ Highest of Angels (twin)

A twin of Metatron is one of the two twins who were once human but have since ascended to heaven. He connects you to the Tree of Life. He makes us aware of our connection to both earth and heaven. Sandalphon was once human; he understands your weaknesses and fragility. He is the energy link between man and spirit, so his energy is swift and decisive. He is a messenger, bringing news from the divine who will connect with your destiny correctly and with precision.

**Archangel Uriel** ~ The light of God

Archangel Uriel seeks to empower and enlighten you. He is a channel for higher wisdom and learning. Call on Archangel Uriel when you need to elevate your soul and spirituality. Archangel Uriel owl is an eccentric; he has a love for innovation and creative solutions. He feels that perception is everything; thinking outside the box lights a path towards realizing your goals. This Angel is self-sufficient, practical, and rational. He is generally interested in being of service in your world. He has a sense of humor and leaves curious signs that capture your interest and guide your path forward.

## Archangel Zadkiel ~ The righteousness of God

Zadkiel helps us with forgiveness and healing. He reminds us of the past and present, allowing us to understand and accept milestones in our life's journey. He gives us the strength to confront our wounds, and he also reminds us to be grateful and appreciates the gifts which surround our daily lives. His energy is gentle, subtle, and inspirational. His words are always calm and sympathetic. He teaches us to accept others, gain an understanding of different perspectives, and forgive. Zadkiel helps you with emotional healing and forgiveness or to remove emotional blocks, whether it relates to yourself or forgiving someone else.

Time set to Coordinated Universal Time Zone (UT±0)

I've noted Meteor Showers on the date they peak.

# JANUARY

| Sun | Mon | Tue | Wed | Thu | Fri | Sat |
|-----|-----|-----|-----|-----|-----|-----|
|     |     |     |     |     |     | 1   |
| 2   | 3   | 4   | 5   | 6   | 7   | 8   |
| 9   | 10  | 11  | 12  | 13  | 14  | 15  |
| 16  | 17  | 18  | 19  | 20  | 21  | 22  |
| 23  | 24  | 25  | 26  | 27  | 28  | 29  |
| 30  | 31  |     |     |     |     |     |

# January Astrology

2nd - New Moon in Capricorn 18:33

3rd - Quadrantids Meteor Shower. January 1st-5th.

7th - Mercury at Greatest Eastern Elongation

9th - First Quarter Moon in Aries 18:11

14th - Mercury Retrograde begins in Aquarius

17th - Wolf Moon. Full Moon in Cancer 23:48

25th - Last Quarter Moon Scorpio 13:42

_____

_____

_____

_____

_____

_____

# New Moon

# WOLF MOON

**31 Friday**

**1 Saturday** ~ New Year's Day

**2 Sunday** ~ New Moon in Capricorn 18:33

Archangel Uriel says that this week brings an increasing focus on developing your life purpose. Getting involved with growing your world brings substance and progression into your life. It brings a focus on self-development. It takes you towards a journey that offers brighter energy as the winds of change blow inspiration into your world. You discover off-the-beaten-track pathways that provide progress. It helps you create tangibles results using your inherent gifts and talents. Actively tapping into the potential possible helps grow your life outwardly towards new assignments. Improvement is looming overhead, and this brings personal goals to the forefront. It has you dreaming big about the possibilities.

**3 Monday** ~ Quadrantids Meteor Shower runs Jan 1 – 5

**4 Tuesday**

**5 Wednesday**

**6 Thursday**

**7 Friday** ~ Mercury at Greatest Eastern Elongation

**8 Saturday**

**9 Sunday** ~ First Quarter Moon in Aries 18:11

Archangel Jophiel says that your willingness to be open to new people and possibilities draws a pleasing result. Something special is brewing in the background of your life. It brings developments that sow the seeds to nurture a dream. News arrives that brings a stroke of good fortune and expansion into your world. Being proactive let you unearth curious opportunities suitable for progression. You land in a landscape ready to blossom into a meaningful journey forward. Life ahead opens a bountiful opportunity to progress a situation forward. It draws a rising aspect to your social life that ushers in new potential.

**10 Monday**

**11 Tuesday**

**12 Wednesday**

**13 Thursday**

**14 Friday** ~ Mercury Retrograde begins in Aquarius

**15 Saturday**

**16 Sunday**

Archangel Gabriel says that you begin developing an area of interest with a clear head and an open mind. It draws a time of adventure and discovery that gets the ball rolling on manifesting positive outcomes. It connects with a social aspect that brings renewal and rejuvenation to your foundations. It kicks off a time of social engagement that draws outings out with friends. Lively conversations offer a thoughtful dialogue that blends new ideas with fresh potential. Engaging with a broader world of support in your life is the ticket to an engaging chapter ahead. Your life heads towards an uptick of potential, bringing refinement, movement, and growth. It redefines what you thought was possible.

**17 Monday** ~ Martin Luther King Day
Full Moon in Cancer 23:48
Wolf Moon

**18 Tuesday**

**19 Wednesday**

**20 Thursday**

**21 Friday**

**22 Saturday**

**23 Sunday**

Angel Metatron reveals that unique possibilities reawaken the creativity within your spirit this week. New ideas and information bring a burst of inspiration flowing into your world that reinvigorates your foundations from the ground up. It gets a chance to use your abilities and grow your talents into new areas. It offers a unique learning experience and brings rising prospects. It provides a stable phase of developing goals ahead. Changes ahead get the inspiration flowing into your life. A focus on building your dreams draws a pleasing result. Immersing yourself in an exciting area gives purpose and substance to your world. It helps set up a long-term structure around your home life.

**24 Monday**

**25 Tuesday** ~ Last Quarter Moon Scorpio 13:42

**26 Wednesday**

**27 Thursday**

**28 Friday**

**29 Saturday**

**30 Sunday**

Angel Raguel confirms that speaking your truth and standing up for your rights is imperative in achieving the highest result possible for your life. If you sense injustice around your life, know that your noble heart can overcome barriers and achieve a positive outcome. It takes you on a path that balances and restores harmony as you know you are doing the right thing. Being impartial and speaking up for what is right draws a sense of justice into your world. Curious changes ahead shift your focus forward. It brings a pivotal time that launches a fresh cycle of growth. You have a lot going on in your life at this time as it brings new options ripe for progression.

# FEBRUARY

| Sun | Mon | Tue | Wed | Thu | Fri | Sat |
|-----|-----|-----|-----|-----|-----|-----|
|     |     | 1   | 2   | 3   | 4   | 5   |
| 6   | 7   | 8   | 9   | 10  | 11  | 12  |
| 13  | 14  | 15  | 16  | 17  | 18  | 19  |
| 20  | 21  | 22  | 23  | 24  | 25  | 26  |
| 27  | 28  |     |     |     |     |     |

# FEBRUARY ASTROLOGY

1ST - NEW MOON IN AQUARIUS 05:45

1ST - CHINESE NEW YEAR (TIGER)

1ST - IMBOLC

4TH - MERCURY RETROGRADE ENDS IN CAPRICORN

8TH - FIRST QUARTER MOON IN TAURUS 13:50

16TH - MERCURY AT GREATEST WESTERN ELONGATION

16TH - SNOW MOON. FULL MOON IN LEO 16:57

23RD - LAST QUARTER MOON IN SCORPIO 22:32

# NEW MOON

# SNOW MOON

**31 Monday**

**1 Tuesday** ~ New Moon in Aquarius 05:45
Chinese New Year (Tiger)
Imbolc

**2 Wednesday**~ Groundhog Day

**3 Thursday**

**4 Friday** ~ Mercury Retrograde ends in Capricorn

**5 Saturday**

**6 Sunday**

Archangel Raziel says that this week reveals a time ripe with possibility. Setting intentions and aspirations is a decisive step in nurturing this vision and demonstrating the potential possible. It brings harmony into focus as it connects you with a broader social environment that supports well-being and abundance. A situation you nurture blossoms into a powerful journey forward for your life. It brings an extraordinary time that releases heaviness and brings joy flowing into your world. It helps you reawaken to the vibrant landscape of potential that surrounds your life.

**7 Monday**

**8 Tuesday** ~ First Quarter Moon in Taurus 13:50

**9 Wednesday**

**10 Thursday**

**11 Friday**

**12 Saturday**

**13 Sunday**

Angel Chamuel shares that a social aspect ahead draws harmony and well-being into your life. It brings a time connected to magic and opportunity as it nurtures interpersonal bonds and supports growth and expansion. It enriches your life as it brings an influx of social opportunities to connect with friends and family. It jumpstarts a journey that speaks to your heart and brings inspiration flowing into your world. Exploring the synergy with someone you care about nurtures well-being and harmony in your life. It tempts you to move out of your comfort zone and embrace a forward-facing journey that offers room to progress into a meaningful path forward.

**14 Monday** ~ Valentine's Day

**15 Tuesday**

**16 Wednesday** ~ Mercury at Greatest Western Elongation
Full Moon in Leo 16:57
Snow Moon.

**17 Thursday**

**18 Friday**

**19 Saturday**

**20 Sunday**

Archangel Ariel reveals that a social aspect ahead helps open your life to new people and possibilities. It brings a cycle of good fortune that kicks off a chapter of progressing your social life. It highlights a new companion who enters your life with wisdom and grace. It brings a productive and adventurous time where significant change is possible. Improving your circumstances is a theme that resonates soundly over the coming weeks. It brings goals to work towards, and many possibilities flow into your world; each represents something new on offer. It brings a time of personal growth that enriches your life.

**21 Monday** ~ Presidents' Day

**22 Tuesday**

**23 Wednesday** ~ Last Quarter Moon in Scorpio 22:32

**24 Thursday**

**25 Friday**

**26 Saturday**

**27 Sunday**

Angel Metatron shares that an attractive avenue opens, and this generates possibilities that inspire creativity and inspiration. The pace of life picks up; it brings an active and productive environment. You thrive under this dynamic sky. It brings expansion, and you begin to trust in the process of developing your life. It brings a peak chapter for innovation, growth, and good fortune. Your social life picks up steam. Invitations flow into your world, drawing a sense of abundance. Lively discussions bring new information to light. It helps you claim your confidence back as you adopt a proactive mindset and develop your dreams. Creativity soars under this powerful positive influence. It brings a new landscape into view.

# MARCH

| Sun | Mon | Tue | Wed | Thu | Fri | Sat |
|-----|-----|-----|-----|-----|-----|-----|
|     |     | 1   | 2   | 3   | 4   | 5   |
| 6   | 7   | 8   | 9   | 10  | 11  | 12  |
| 13  | 14  | 15  | 16  | 17  | 18  | 19  |
| 20  | 21  | 22  | 23  | 24  | 25  | 26  |
| 27  | 28  |     |     |     |     |     |

# MARCH ASTROLOGY

2ND - NEW MOON IN PISCES 17:34

10TH - FIRST QUARTER MOON IN GEMINI 10:45

18TH - WORM MOON. FULL MOON IN VIRGO 07:17

20TH - OSTARA/SPRING EQUINOX 15:33

25TH - LAST QUARTER MOON IN CAPRICORN 05:37

# NEW MOON

# WORM MOON

**28 Monday**

**1 Tuesday Shrove** ~ Tuesday (Mardi Gras)

**2 Wednesday** ~ Ash Wednesday Lent Begins
New Moon in Pisces 17:34

**3 Thursday**

**4 Friday**

**5 Saturday**

**6 Sunday**

Archangel Zadkiel feels that you are on the right path towards developing your life. It brings a time that is supportive and focuses on building stable foundations. It brings a strong focus on nurturing an emotional bond which hits a special note in your social life. Improving this area draws opportunities that connect you with a wellspring of abundance. It lets you release the stress and doubt and feel confident that your journey is evolving to a new level of potential. Improvements around communication bring an enriching phase to light. It brings lighter energy that draws inspiration and joy.

**7 Monday**

**8 Tuesday**

**9 Wednesday**

**10 Thursday** ~ First Quarter Moon in Gemini 10:45

**11 Friday**

**12 Saturday**

**13 Sunday**

Archangel Uriel shares that new possibilities ahead light the fire in your belly. It sparks a journey that flings outworn energy to the curb. Confidence rises, leading the way towards developing a new endeavor. Working with your talents puts the shine on abilities and creates a stable basis from which to build your dreams. A clue ahead reveals an option that blossoms into a journey worth growing. It brings a time of dynamic activity that offers steady growth. A new assignment brings gifts that unpack a new chapter of potential. It speaks of further information ahead that stirs the pot of potential. It helps you manifest a potent brew of options worth developing.

**14 Monday**

**15 Tuesday**

**16 Wednesday** ~ Purim (Begins at sundown)

**17 Thursday** ~ Purim (Ends at sunset)
St Patrick's Day

**18 Friday** ~ Full Moon in Virgo 07:17

**19 Saturday**

**20 Sunday** ~ Ostara/Spring Equinox 15:33

Angel Sandalphon reveals that a fresh cycle beckons; it leads to possibilities that inspire your life on all levels. Your willingness to push boundaries back is fundamental in demonstrating the highest potential possible. It brings a journey worth developing as it grows your abilities in critical areas that extend your reach into new options. It brings a journey that advances your skills and has your life moving towards a unique assignment. It draws a chapter of growth and prosperity as you harness adaptability, innovation, and creativity to achieve a pleasing result for your life. It opens a groundbreaking chapter that sees optimism and inspiration surging.

**21 Monday**

**22 Tuesday**

**23 Wednesday**

**24 Thursday**

**25 Friday** ~ Last Quarter Moon in Capricorn 05:37

**26 Saturday**

**27 Sunday**

Angel Gabriel says that working with your abilities brings a purposeful chapter that offers happiness and connection. It creates space to focus on your life and make your goals a priority. A peak of creative energy ahead draws inspiration and possibility. It brings the magic and excitement flowing into your world as it takes you towards a highly expressive and creative landscape. It brings a bountiful chapter that sets the stage to grow a dream. Fortune shines brightly overhead. It does swing things in your favor as you land in an area that offers room to progress your skills and abilities forward. It brings a fruitful time that builds stable foundations that provide a secure platform for growing your vision for future growth.

# MARCH

## 28 Monday

## 29 Tuesday

## 30 Wednesday

## 31 Thursday

# APRIL

| Sun | Mon | Tue | Wed | Thu | Fri | Sat |
|-----|-----|-----|-----|-----|-----|-----|
|     |     |     |     |     | 1   | 2   |
| 3   | 4   | 5   | 6   | 7   | 8   | 9   |
| 10  | 11  | 12  | 13  | 14  | 15  | 16  |
| 17  | 18  | 19  | 20  | 21  | 22  | 23  |
| 24  | 25  | 26  | 27  | 28  | 29  | 30  |

# April Astrology

1st - New Moon in Aries 06:24

9th - First Quarter Moon in Cancer 06:47

16th - Pink Moon. Full Moon in Libra 18:54

22nd - Lyrids Meteor Shower from April 16-25

23rd - Last Quarter Moon in Aquarius 11:56.

29th - Mercury Greatest Eastern Elongation of 20.6 degrees from the Sun.

30th - New Moon in Taurus 20:27

_____

_____

_____

_____

_____

_____

# New Moon

# PINK MOON

_____

_____

_____

_____

_____

_____

_____

**1 Friday** ~ All Fools/April Fool's Day
New Moon in Aries 06:24

**2 Saturday** ~ Ramadan Begins

**3 Sunday**

Angel Chamuel shares that change overhead takes you on a new adventure. It sees improvements in terms of friendship, creativity, and networking. It lets you plot a course that helps you tackle new dreams and goals. A surge of inspiration flows into your social life. It sets the stage to connect with others in your broader community. It brings a time filled with music, laughter, and vibrant conversations. It brings a resourceful and creative path towards expanding your talents and working with your abilities to achieve the highest result possible in your life.

**4 Monday**

**5 Tuesday**

**6 Wednesday**

**7 Thursday**

**22 Friday** ~ Lyrids Meteor Shower from April 16-25
Passover (ends at sunset)
Orthodox Good Friday
Earth Day

**23 Saturday** ~ Last Quarter Moon in Aquarius 11:56

**24 Sunday** ~ Orthodox Easter

Angel Raphael shares that this week is a time to expand the boundaries of your life. As you unfurl the coming chapter, you discover lightness and engagement with a social aspect. It brings a unique possibility to the forefront of your life. You benefit from mingling and networking with friends and companions. As foundations stabilize, you unlock the gate and head towards greener pastures. It helps you move away from what has been a stormy backdrop and move towards developing an area of interest. Fantastic possibilities blossom under your nurturing touch. Favorable changes are coming up. It kicks off a social environment that beckons you to expand your horizons. It brings an environment ahead that shifts your focus towards mingling and networking.

**25 Monday**

**26 Tuesday**

**27 Wednesday**

**28 Thursday**

# MAY

| Sun | Mon | Tue | Wed | Thu | Fri | Sat |
|-----|-----|-----|-----|-----|-----|-----|
| 1 | 2 | 3 | 4 | 5 | 6 | 7 |
| 8 | 9 | 10 | 11 | 12 | 13 | 14 |
| 15 | 16 | 17 | 18 | 19 | 20 | 21 |
| 22 | 23 | 24 | 25 | 26 | 27 | 28 |
| 29 | 30 | 31 | | | | |

# May Astrology

6th - Eta Aquarids Meteor Shower, April 19th - May 28th

9th - First Quarter Moon in Leo 00:21

10th - Mercury Retrograde begins in Gemini

16th - Total Lunar Eclipse 01:32

16th - Flower Moon. Full Moon in Scorpio 04:13

22nd - Last Quarter Moon in Aquarius 18:43

30th - New Quarter Moon in Leo 00:21

_____

_____

_____

_____

_____

_____

_____

# NEW MOON

# FLOWER MOON

**29 Friday** ~ Mercury Greatest Eastern Elongation of 20.6 degrees from the Sun.

**30 Saturday** ~ Partial Solar Eclipse
New Moon in Taurus 20:27

**1 Sunday** ~ Beltane/May Day
Ramadan Ends

Angel Uriel says mischievously to watch for a sign that provides a curious clue ahead. It brings a lead that sees you working with your talents and refining your skills. It lets you integrate change sustainability to achieve a grounded foundation from which to grow your life outwardly. Things turn a corner, and you soon get busy in a dynamic environment. It brings a new role on offer that advances your life forward. It creates a heightened sense of security that gives you the stability needed to grow your life. It sets the stage to take in new levels of growth and advancement in your working life. Your career goes from strength to strength as you extend your reach into this prominent area. Any issues currently on the periphery of your working life disperse.

**2 Monday**

**3 Tuesday**

**4 Wednesday**

**5 Thursday**

**6 Friday** ~ Eta Aquarids Meteor Shower April 19th - May 28th

**7 Saturday**

**8 Sunday** ~ Mother's Day

Angel Jophiel shares that you can honor your wild and rebellious tendencies and embrace the path that calls you. Heeding the yearning within your heart stokes the fires of inspiration. A passionate approach ahead opens to diversity, creativity, and success. It is a journey that unearths hidden gems of possibility. Sifting and sorting through the various options help you come up with a winner. It lets you create clear goals that mark the right way forward. Taking down barriers harnesses the sense of manifestation that offers new territory and an expansive view to contemplate. A highly creative and self-expressive phase is looming. You set sail on a voyage that provides happiness and self-development.

MAY

**9 Monday** ~ First Quarter Moon in Leo 00:21

**10 Tuesday** ~ Mercury Retrograde begins in Gemini.

**11 Wednesday**

**12 Thursday**

**13 Friday**

**14 Saturday**

**15 Sunday**

Angel Raphael says that the social aspect ahead lifts the lid on new opportunities. It brings a busy time that offers a foundation worth growing. It will seem like you've opened the window and let the fresh air flow into your world. It brings a time that rules expansion, and this brings plenty of opportunities to explore. Being open to new people and situations sweetens your journey. It marks a time that is inspired and adventurous. It sees you gliding forward as you capture the essence of enthusiasm and merge your dreams with reality. A fortunate trend arrives that blends beautifully with your aspirations for future growth. It lets you make strides in improving your circumstances and navigating the path ahead with efficiency and grace.

**16 Monday** ~ Full Moon in Scorpio 04:13
Total Lunar Eclipse 01:32
Flower Moon

**17 Tuesday**

**18 Wednesday**

**19 Thursday**

**20 Friday**

**21 Saturday**

**22 Sunday** ~ Last Quarter Moon in Aquarius 18:43

Archangel Gabriel says that life has been a battle, but you will shift gears soon and face the Sun. It helps you turn a corner and draw a positive influence into your life. She says to cherish the warmth of friends and enjoy every moment. An aspect ahead brings the answers to your more critical life questions. It opens a path that lets you channel your energy into an area of interest. It brings an engaging time of social interaction and friendly banter that adds playful energy into your life. It does have you dreaming big about the possibilities when you open your life to new people and experiences. It brings an active environment of mingling that offers enriching energy.

# MAY

**23 Monday** ~ Victoria Day (Canada)

**24 Tuesday**

**25 Wednesday**

**26 Thursday**

**27 Friday**

**28 Saturday**

**29 Sunday**

Angel Jeremiel says that listening to your emotions taps into the correct path. It lets you show your talents to a broader audience and has you exploring new pathways of growth and prosperity. Fortune shines upon your life as you transition towards a positive chapter that expands your horizons into new areas. News arrives that brings balance and harmony into your life. It brings a time of expansion, creativity, and adventure. Your ability to manifest positive outcomes heightens, and this reveals the type of advancement that is heartening. It enriches your world and gives you a clear indication you are free to follow your heart and grow your life outwardly. As you plot your course forward, you better understand what happens when you set the bar higher.

# JUNE

| Sun | Mon | Tue | Wed | Thu | Fri | Sat |
|-----|-----|-----|-----|-----|-----|-----|
|     |     |     | 1   | 2   | 3   | 4   |
| 5   | 6   | 7   | 8   | 9   | 10  | 11  |
| 12  | 13  | 14  | 15  | 16  | 17  | 18  |
| 19  | 20  | 21  | 22  | 23  | 24  | 25  |
| 26  | 27  | 28  | 29  | 30  |     |     |

# June Astrology

3rd - Mercury Retrograde ends in Taurus

7th - First Quarter Moon in Virgo 14:48

14th - Strawberry Moon. Full Moon in Sagittarius Supermoon 11:51

16th - Mercury's greatest Western elongation of 23.2 degrees from the Sun

21st - Last Quarter Moon in Aries 03:11

21st - Midsummer/Litha Solstice 09:13

29th - New Moon in Cancer 02:52

# NEW MOON

# STRAWBERRY MOON

**30 Monday** ~ New Moon in Gemini 11:30
Memorial Day

**31 Tuesday**

**1 Wednesday**

**2 Thursday**

**3 Friday** ~ Mercury Retrograde ends in Taurus

**4 Saturday** ~ Shavuot (Begins at sunset)

**5 Sunday**

Angel Azrael comes calling this week to say that beautiful symmetry is coming, drawing healing and closure into your world. It brings the energy that is quite therapeutic for your mood as it offers lightness and harmony. It forms the basis of grounded energy from which you can expand your life. Consequently, you head towards an uptick of potential that offers new leads ripe for development. Shedding outworn areas resolves the issues that have limited progress. It cracks the code to a brighter chapter ahead. It gives you the green light to connect with inspiration and creativity. A surprise arrives that bolsters your mood. It brings a new friendship to light and lets you become involved in mingling and socializing.

**6 Monday** ~ Shavuot (Ends at sunset)

**7 Tuesday** ~ First Quarter Moon in Virgo 14:48

**8 Wednesday**

**9 Thursday**

**10 Friday**

**11 Saturday**

**12 Sunday**

Angel Haniel shares that opportunity comes knocking soon. It brings a chapter of soul-stirring conversations shared with friends. It ushers in thoughtful discussions that balance bonds and enriches your spirit. It brings expansion to your circle of friends as a new companion pops into view. It brings lively discussions with an engaging character. You foster a bond that draws meaning and connection. It brings a supportive time that focuses on sharing thoughts and communication with someone insightful and wise. Expanding your vision brings options that remove the heaviness and lets the light in your life. It brings rapid improvements and an environment that is active and productive. Life becomes brighter as greener pastures beckon and tempt you onward.

**13 Monday**

**14 Tuesday** ~ Full Moon in Sagittarius, Supermoon 11:51
Strawberry Moon.
Flag Day

**15 Wednesday**

**16 Thursday** ~ Mercury's greatest Western elongation of 23.2 degrees from the Sun

**17 Friday**

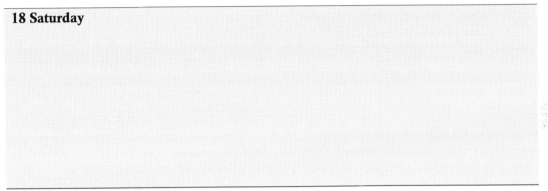

**18 Saturday**

**19 Sunday** ~ Father's Day

Archangel Chamuel says that new possibilities ahead bring news that lifts the barriers. It opens your life to a social aspect that draws harmony and joy. It lets you resolve outworn energy as you head towards a turning point that offers rising prospects. It brings a lighter, happier phase of focusing on an area that holds meaning. Positive influences a surge in your social life and get a heightened sense of security that nurtures well-being and stability. It begins an expressive chapter that focuses on people and bonds. It brings lively discussions to the forefront of your life.

**20 Monday**

**21 Tuesday** ~ Midsummer/Litha Solstice. 09:13
Last Quarter Moon in Aries 03:11

**22 Wednesday**

**23 Thursday**

**24 Friday**

**25 Saturday**

**26 Sunday**

Angel Raphael feels you get a chance to get involved with a curious project that offers a collaborative approach. It brings an engaging and supportive environment. It has you focusing on something fresh and creatively stimulating. Constructive dialogue stimulate new ideas that bring a lively time of sharing with friends. It ignites the fires of inspiration and draws a happy chapter to light the way forward. The benefits ahead get something to celebrate. It does bring the curtain up on a fresh chapter that places you center stage to improve your world.

**27 Monday**

**28 Tuesday**

**29 Wednesday** ~ New Moon in Cancer 02:52

**30 Thursday**

# JULY

| Sun | Mon | Tue | Wed | Thu | Fri | Sat |
|-----|-----|-----|-----|-----|-----|-----|
|     |     |     |     |     | 1   | 2   |
| 3   | 4   | 5   | 6   | 7   | 8   | 9   |
| 10  | 11  | 12  | 13  | 14  | 15  | 16  |
| 17  | 18  | 19  | 20  | 21  | 22  | 23  |
| 24  | 25  | 26  | 27  | 28  | 29  | 30  |

## July Astrology

7th - First Quarter Moon in Libra 02:14

13th - Buck Moon. Full Moon in Capricorn. Supermoon 18:37

20th - Last Quarter Moon in Aries 14:18

28th - New Moon in Leo 17:54

28th - Delta Aquarids Meteor Shower. July 12th - August 23rd

# New Moon

# Buck Moon

**1 Friday** ~ Canada Day

**2 Saturday**

**3 Sunday**

Angel Gabrielle speaks of an opportunity ahead that allows you to showcase your talents. It offers a carefree time that heightens creativity and brings new projects and assignments worthy of your attention. It offers a busy and active environment where you can build your life outwardly. You are on the cusp of change, and a breakthrough ahead marks the right direction to go down. It speaks of new possibilities ahead that place you in an enviable position. A lucky break brings a cheerful glow to your life. It puts a spring in your step as new possibilities bring light energy into your life.

**4 Monday** ~ Independence Day

**5 Tuesday**

**6 Wednesday**

**7 Thursday** ~ First Quarter Moon in Libra 02:14

**8 Friday**

**9 Saturday**

**10 Sunday**

Archangel Chamuel shares that you discover a lucky break that offers happy surprises and a joyous time spent with friends. It provides a creative aspect that draws communication, ideas, and brainstorming sessions. Supportive energy brings a considerable boost into your life as the possibility of new assignments glimmers overhead. It's just the right kind of setting to dabble in a new interest and tap into your creative side. Sharing your gifts with a broader audience offers valuable results. It brings a journey that grows your abilities and advances your talents into virgin territory.

**11 Monday**

**12 Tuesday**

**13 Wednesday** ~ Full Moon in Capricorn, Supermoon 18:37
Buck Moon

**14 Thursday**

**15 Friday**

**16 Saturday**

**17 Sunday**

Archangel Raguel says that helpful news arrives soon. It removes limiting beliefs and ushers in a prosperous phase of developing a dream. Focused and determined, you unearth new leads that take your abilities forward. It brings a time of building a secure foundation and progressing towards growing your career path. It gets an upgrade that may feel subtle at first but soon opens pathways towards growth. It brings balance and stability, and this becomes the basis from which you advance your abilities forward. It enables a bold move into new areas.

**18 Monday**

**19 Tuesday**

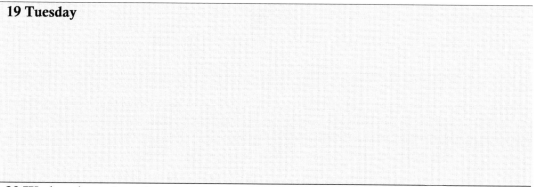

**20 Wednesday** ~ Last Quarter Moon in Aries 14:18

**21 Thursday**

**22 Friday**

**23 Saturday**

**24 Sunday**

Archangel Raphael shares that change is in the air, and it has you dreaming about the possibilities when you meet someone who connects with your heart space. You link up with someone who seeks a similar destination. It brings a time of pushing back boundaries and challenging your beliefs with new information. It shifts your attention to deepening a bond that offers room to promote harmony in your personal life. It draws lively discussions that inspire growth. A heartfelt conversation cracks the code to developing your future life.

**25 Monday**

**26 Tuesday**

**27 Wednesday**

**28 Thursday** ~ Delta Aquarids Meteor Shower. July 12th – August 23rd
New Moon in Leo 17:54

**29 Friday** ~ Islamic New Year

**30 Saturday**

**31 Sunday**

Archangel Jeremiel says that life becomes a whirlwind positively as it brings a boost into your life. It lights an appealing path forward. Change is forecast for your life. Life becomes happier and more expansive as you push back the barriers and embrace a more social and connected environment. Sharing with friends and companions rebalances and renews your energy. It brings a significant improvement to your social life that offers a chance to nurture a bond with someone who is engaging and attentive. It brings lively discussions ahead. You touch down on a landscape ripe with options.

# AUGUST

| Sun | Mon | Tue | Wed | Thu | Fri | Sat |
|-----|-----|-----|-----|-----|-----|-----|
|     | 1   | 2   | 3   | 4   | 5   | 6   |
| 7   | 8   | 9   | 10  | 11  | 12  | 13  |
| 14  | 15  | 16  | 17  | 18  | 19  | 20  |
| 21  | 22  | 23  | 24  | 25  | 26  | 27  |
| 28  | 29  | 30  | 31  |     |     |     |

# August Astrology

5TH - First Quarter Moon Scorpio 11:06

8TH - Full Moon in Aquarius Supermoon 01:35. Sturgeon Moon.

8TH - Perseids Meteor Shower July 17th - August 24th

14TH - Saturn at Opposition

19TH - Last Quarter Moon in Taurus 04:36

27TH - New Moon in Virgo 08:16

27TH - Mercury at Greatest Eastern Elongation at 27.3 degrees from the Sun

_____

_____

_____

_____

_____

_____

## NEW MOON

# STURGEON MOON

# AUGUST

**1 Monday** ~ Lammas/Lughnasadh

**2 Tuesday**

**3 Wednesday**

**4 Thursday**

**5 Friday** ~ First Quarter Moon Scorpio 11:06

**6 Saturday**

**7 Sunday**

Angel Metatron says that you move in a direction that triggers a cascade of exciting potential. It brings the magic coursing into your life as your instincts spot a diamond in the rough. Getting involved with this area puts a shine on your talents. Fascinating opportunities emerge that opens the gateway forward. It brings news and excitement flowing into your life and sets the stage for a new adventure. Chasing your dreams, you embrace a journey that enhances creativity and expands your energy. You reveal an option that brings a boost to your world as it highlights a path of self-discovery and self-development. It offers smooth sailing towards calmer waters.

**8 Monday**

**9 Tuesday**

**10 Wednesday**

**11 Thursday**

**12 Friday** ~ Perseids Meteor Shower July 17th - August 24th
Full Moon in Aquarius, Supermoon 01:35
Sturgeon Moon

**13 Saturday**

**14 Sunday** ~ Saturn at Opposition

Archangel Uriel feels that you are disciplined enough to study a course that elevates your abilities. A profession that provides an effective forum to exert your influence on those around you would be ideal. An educator or entertainer, for instance. You have a strong drive to succeed that enables actions to turn into tangible results. It blesses your life with reserves of endurance, vision, and resourcefulness. In terms of manifestation, your abilities are growing. It opens a bevy of possibilities that offer growth and progression. Life brightens under a bright sky that sees magic bloom in your world.

**15 Monday**

**16 Tuesday**

**17 Wednesday**

**18 Thursday**

**19 Friday** ~ Last Quarter Moon in Taurus 04:36

**20 Saturday**

**21 Sunday**

Archangel Sandalphon says that a shift ahead that wonderfully moves you. It has you moving in alignment with the person you are becoming. It opens a path that releases the heaviness and offers a time for developing goals. If you look at moving home, there will be options to explore that draw excitement into your life. It lets you make tracks on redesigning your home life and improving your circumstances from the ground up. It brings a time of sharing thoughts and discussions with a kindred spirit who inspires. Your care and attention to detail are instrumental in nurturing a closer bond. It brings an optimistic phase that lets you make headway on developing personal goals with an attentive and engaging person.

## AUGUST

**22 Monday**

**23 Tuesday**

**24 Wednesday**

**25 Thursday**

**26 Friday**

**27 Saturday** ~ Mercury at Greatest Eastern Elongation at 27.3 degrees from the Sun
New Moon in Virgo 08:16

**28 Sunday**

Archangel Ariel reveals that your social life heads to an upswing. It lights up pathways of connectedness and self-expression. You open a gateway that brings new potential into your world. It's a fast-moving social environment that offers new friendships. It does see a companion ahead who plays a significant role in future events. As you expand your horizons and bring new people into your life, you discover that other situations fall by the wayside. It lets you streamline your energy and focus on the areas that hold the most significant meaning. You evolve and reach a new level of understanding about your life and the path ahead.

# September

| Sun | Mon | Tue | Wed | Thu | Fri | Sat |
|-----|-----|-----|-----|-----|-----|-----|
|     |     |     |     | 1   | 2   | 3   |
| 4   | 5   | 6   | 7   | 8   | 9   | 10  |
| 11  | 12  | 13  | 14  | 15  | 16  | 17  |
| 18  | 19  | 20  | 21  | 22  | 23  | 24  |
| 25  | 26  | 27  | 28  | 29  | 30  |     |

138

## September Astrology

7TH - FIRST QUARTER MOON SAGITTARIUS 18:08

10TH - MERCURY RETROGRADE BEGINS IN LIBRA

10TH - CORN MOON. HARVEST MOON. FULL MOON IN PISCES 09:58

16TH - NEPTUNE AT OPPOSITION

17TH - LAST QUARTER MOON IN GEMINI 21:52

23 - MABON/FALL EQUINOX. 01:03

25TH - NEW MOON IN LIBRA 21:54

26TH - JUPITER AT OPPOSITION

## New Moon

_____

_____

_____

_____

_____

_____

_____

## Corn/Harvest Moon

**29 Monday**

**30 Tuesday**

**31 Wednesday**

**1 Thursday**

**2 Friday**

**3 Saturday** ~ First Quarter Moon Sagittarius 18:08

**4 Sunday**

Archangel Raziel is pleased to share that life brings a time of increasing stability that improves your social life. It brings beautiful changes that give you the green light to move forward towards deepening this bond. Life supports your vision as things fall into place with a sense of synchronicity. It beautifully orients your thoughts towards romance and adventure. Overall, life moves towards a busy and exciting time exploring the synergy with someone who captures your interest. It rewards with a fresh slate of potential that reveals a sunny sky overhead. The essence of manifestation helps guide this situation forward.

**5 Monday** ~ Labor Day

**6 Tuesday**

**7 Wednesday**

**8 Thursday**

**9 Friday**

**10 Saturday** ~ Mercury Retrograde begins in Libra.
Full Moon in Pisces 09:58
Corn Moon. Harvest Moon

**11 Sunday**

Archangel Gabriel out is excited to share that Things head to an upswing soon. Life offers new possibilities that draw stability and balance into your world. It helps you navigate forward towards greener pastures. Making yourself a priority brings a turning point as it connects you to people who support your growth and evolution. It opens the door to revolution and renewal. The strength in your spirit offers the ability to push back barriers and create a bridge towards a brighter chapter. News ahead brings a powerful boost into your world.

**12 Monday**

**13 Tuesday**

**14 Wednesday**

**15 Thursday**

**16 Friday** ~ Neptune at Opposition

**17 Saturday** ~ Last Quarter Moon in Gemini 21:52

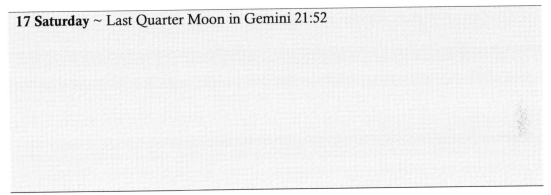

**18 Sunday**

Archangel Raphael says that a unique aspect ahead brings new people into your life. A path of abundance opens that hits a high note in your social life. Something is brewing that brings a transition towards an exciting journey of nurturing bonds. It lets you pick up the threads of manifestation and weave a basket of connections that supports growth and well-being. It offers a social environment that adds magic and glamour to your life. It closes the door on outworn areas that drain your energy; creating a stable foundation is the first step in making your mark on a brighter chapter ahead.

**19 Monday**

**20 Tuesday**

**21 Wednesday**~ International Day of Peace

**22 Thursday**

**23 Friday** ~ Mabon/Fall Equinox. 01:03

**24 Saturday**

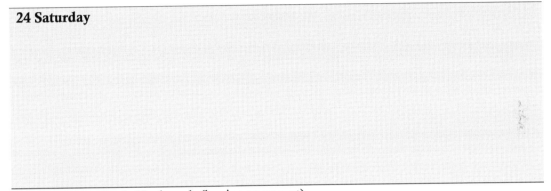

**25 Sunday** ~ Rosh Hashanah (begins at sunset)
New Moon in Libra 21:54

Archangel Haniel whispers that a changing scene on the horizon brings new potential into your social life. It connects you with kindred spirits, and this creates space to focus on developing ambitious goals. It brings a happy chapter that broadens your social circle. Abundance flourishes as you reveal new information that brings exciting options to light. Good energy flows easily and naturally around your life. She says that luck is your faithful companion as it brings good fortune swirling around the periphery of your vision. It places you in the proper alignment to extend your reach into new areas and connect with kindred spirits who have a heartfelt message to share with you.

**26 Monday** ~ Jupiter at Opposition

**27 Tuesday** ~ Rosh Hashanah (ends at sunset)

**28 Wednesday**

**29 Thursday**

# OCTOBER

| Sun | Mon | Tue | Wed | Thu | Fri | Sat |
|-----|-----|-----|-----|-----|-----|-----|
|     |     |     |     |     |     | 1   |
| 2   | 3   | 4   | 5   | 6   | 7   | 8   |
| 9   | 10  | 11  | 12  | 13  | 14  | 15  |
| 16  | 17  | 18  | 19  | 20  | 21  | 22  |
| 23  | 24  | 25  | 26  | 27  | 28  | 29  |
| 30  | 31  |     |     |     |     |     |

## October Astrology

2ND - MERCURY RETROGRADE ENDS IN VIRGO

3RD - FIRST QUARTER MOON IN CAPRICORN 00.14

7TH - DRACONIDS METEOR SHOWER. OCT 6TH -10TH

8TH - MERCURY GREATEST WESTERN ELONGATION

9TH - HUNTERS MOON. FULL MOON IN ARIES 20:54

17TH - LAST QUARTER MOON IN CANCER 17.15

21ST -ORIONIDS METEOR SHOWER. OCTOBER 2ND - NOVEMBER 7TH

25TH - NEW MOON IN SCORPIO 10:48

25TH - PARTIAL SOLAR ECLIPSE

# New Moon

## HUNTERS MOON

**30 Friday**

**1 Saturday**

**2 Sunday** ~ Mercury Retrograde ends in Virgo

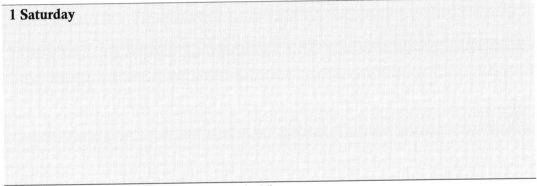

Archangel Michael feels that exploring diverse options supports a journey of growth and evolution. It lets you land in a productive atmosphere that is ripe with potential. Opportunities to mingle set the scene to expand your social life with new friends and companions. It brings a happy chapter that rules a time of expansion and harmony. It brings thoughtful discussions that offer cutting-edge ideas, which blaze a trail towards a path of inspiration. He says that finding your true purpose draws peace and well-being into your world. It brings the motivation to reach for something exceptional, and in your heart, you can know that you can achieve gold.

**3 Monday** ~ First Quarter Moon in Capricorn 00.14

**4 Tuesday** ~ Yom Kippur (begins at sunset)

**5 Wednesday** ~ Yom Kippur (ends at sunset)

**6 Thursday**

**7 Friday** ~ Draconids Meteor Shower. Oct 6-10

**8 Saturday** ~ Mercury Greatest Western Elongation

**9 Sunday** ~ Sukkot (begins at sunset)
Full Moon in Aries 20:54
Hunters Moon

Angel Michael shares that you discover an area that opens the floodgates towards an enterprising chapter of growth and prosperity. Things are on the move during this vital aspect. Life is a blur of operational productivity, and you thrive in a busy and rewarding environment. It is a time that sees you initiating a new endeavor. You launch your ship of dreams and discover possibilities that grow your potential by leaps and bounds. There is a breakthrough that lights a path forward and helps you sustain a sound clip of progress as you reach for a lofty goal.

**10 Monday** ~ Thanksgiving Day (Canada)
Indigenous People's Day
Columbus Day

**11 Tuesday**

**12 Wednesday**

**13 Thursday**

# OCTOBER

**14 Friday**

**15 Saturday**

**16 Sunday** ~ Sukkot (ends at sunset)

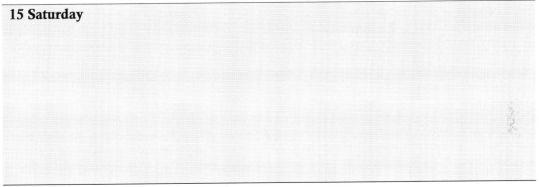

Angel Raziel shares that your creativity is a valuable resource that helps you visualize the path ahead. It brings foundations that draw security. You soon connect with an area that offers you learning and growth. Shining a light on advancing your talents outlines a path that provides prosperity and growth. It brings pathways that grow your abilities. The work undertaken creates a shift that brings a myriad of possibilities into your world. You enter a cycle of increasing abundance that leaves you feeling radiant. It carries news worth celebrating, which puts you in the mood to mingle with your broader social circle. It brings a happy time of socializing and networking with friends and kindred spirits who connect you with your tribe.

**17 Monday** ~ Last Quarter Moon in Cancer 17.15

**18 Tuesday**

**19 Wednesday**

**20 Thursday**

# OCTOBER

**21 Friday** ~ Orionids Meteor Shower. October 2nd - November 7th

**22 Saturday**

**23 Sunday**

Archangel Chamuel says that someone from your past comes calling. When you hear from this person, it cracks the code to a more connected and supported environment. It lets you come up with new options and answers to improve the potential possible with this person. It offers a social aspect that brings news, engagement, and possibility. It adds a buzz of excitement with a dash of adventure to your social life. It brings the fun and joy flowing into your world as you build stable foundations that are grounded and enriching. It underscores a time of change ahead for your life.

**24 Monday**

**25 Tuesday** ~ New Moon in Scorpio 10:48
Partial Solar Eclipse

**26 Wednesday**

**27 Thursday**

**28 Friday**

**29 Saturday**

**30 Sunday**

Angel Zadkiel reveals that harnessing the energy of forgiveness is a powerful tool to improve bonds and harmonize aspects of your social life. It turns the page on a brighter chapter that uses empathy and compassion to draw balance into your surroundings. Resonating forgiveness and kindness is a fantastic way to explore the energy that draws stability and balance into interpersonal bonds. It brings a journey that draws transformation and happiness. It replenishes emotional tanks and draws enriching possibilities into your world. It releases the heaviness and transforms your situation towards a happier chapter.

# NOVEMBER

| Sun | Mon | Tue | Wed | Thu | Fri | Sat |
|-----|-----|-----|-----|-----|-----|-----|
|     |     | 1   | 2   | 3   | 4   | 5   |
| 6   | 7   | 8   | 9   | 10  | 11  | 12  |
| 13  | 14  | 15  | 16  | 17  | 18  | 19  |
| 20  | 21  | 22  | 23  | 24  | 25  | 26  |
| 27  | 28  | 29  | 30  |     |     |     |

# November Astrology

1ST - FIRST QUARTER MOON IN AQUARIUS 06.37

4TH - TAURIDS METEOR SHOWER. SEPTEMBER 7TH - DECEMBER 10TH

8TH - FULL MOON IN TAURUS 11:01 BEAVER MOON.

8TH - TOTAL LUNAR ECLIPSE

9TH - URANUS AT OPPOSITION

16TH - LAST QUARTER MOON IN LEO 13:27

17TH - LEONIDS METEOR SHOWER NOV 6TH-30TH

23RD - NEW MOON IN SAGITTARIUS 22:57

30TH - FIRST QUARTER MOON PISCES 14:36

# NEW MOON

# Beaver Moon

**31 Monday** ~ Samhain/Halloween
All Hallows Eve

**1 Tuesday** ~ First Quarter Moon in Aquarius 06.37
All Saints' Day

**2 Wednesday**

**3 Thursday**

# NOVEMBER

**4 Friday** ~ Taurids Meteor Shower. September 7th - December 10th

**5 Saturday**

**6 Sunday**

Angel Gabriel feels that your willingness to explore innovative options brings a path you can grow. Learning and refining your talents elevates the potential possible. A piece of the puzzle reveals when an opportunity comes knocking with an offer worth exploring. It brings a prosperous cycle that lets you make your stamp on the path ahead. Golden threads of potential swirl around the periphery of your life. Clearing the decks for a fresh chapter, you achieve excellent results by expanding your horizons. There is a social aspect ahead that replenishes the emotional tank.

**7 Monday**

**8 Tuesday** ~ Full Moon in Taurus 11:01
Total Lunar Eclipse
Beaver Moon

**9 Wednesday** ~ Uranus at Opposition

**10 Thursday**

**11 Friday** ~ Remembrance Day (Canada)
Veterans Day

**12 Saturday**

**13 Sunday**

Angel Raziel heightens faith and belief in the divine. He says that adopting a broader perspective holds the key to rebalancing your energy. You soon gain clarity and insight as information arrives that shines a light on improving the situation. It helps you turn a corner and draw peace and stability into your foundations. Letting fixed expectations help you move beyond areas that limit progress. It creates space for new goals and possibilities to emerge. It enables you to break down the hurdles and dive into an empowering phase of new options.

**14 Monday**

**15 Tuesday**

**16 Wednesday** ~ Last Quarter Moon in Leo 13:27

**17 Thursday** ~ Leonids Meteor Shower November 6-30

**18 Friday**

**19 Saturday**

**20 Sunday**

Angel Jophiel says there will be beneficial changes ahead. It brings a social aspect that harmonizes well-being and supports growth. It offers the prospects of developing a bond of the heart, and this inspires change. It brings a dynamic change of pace that nurtures a supportive environment. Things fall into place, bringing space to renew your spirit from the ground up. It brings a path of happiness into focus that reboots and rejuvenates your energy.

**21 Monday**

**22 Tuesday**

**23 Wednesday** ~ New Moon in Sagittarius 22:57

**24 Thursday** ~ Thanksgiving Day (US)

**25 Friday**

**26 Saturday**

**27 Sunday**

Angel Gabriel heightens creativity; she provides understanding and acceptance as you passage forward through life. She says that forgiveness swirls around your life and tempts you towards improving social bonds. It anchors your energy in improving the potential possible. Significant changes overhead connect you with new possibilities that will enhance your world. It brings a social aspect that draws a refreshing change. It connects you to expanding horizons that usher in a chance of healing and re-establishing a bond of meaning.

# December

| Sun | Mon | Tue | Wed | Thu | Fri | Sat |
|-----|-----|-----|-----|-----|-----|-----|
|     |     |     |     | 1   | 2   | 3   |
| 4   | 5   | 6   | 7   | 8   | 9   | 10  |
| 11  | 12  | 13  | 14  | 15  | 16  | 17  |
| 18  | 19  | 20  | 21  | 22  | 23  | 24  |
| 25  | 26  | 27  | 28  | 29  | 30  | 31  |

# December Astrology

8th - Cold Moon. Moon Before Yule

8th - Full Moon in Gemini 04:07

8th - Mars at Opposition

13th - Geminids Meteor Shower. Dec 7th - 17th

16th - Last Quarter Moon in Virgo 08:56

21st - Ursids Meteor Shower December 17 - 25th

21st - Mercury at Greatest Eastern elongation.

21st - Yule/Winter Solstice at 09:48

23rd - New Moon in Capricorn 10:16

29th - Mercury Retrograde begins in Capricorn

30th - First Quarter Moon Aries 01:21

## New Moon

# COLD MOON

**28 Monday**

**29 Tuesday**

**30 Wednesday** ~ First Quarter Moon Pisces 14:36

**1 Thursday**

**2 Friday**

**3 Saturday**

**4 Sunday**

Angel Raphael is pleased to tell you soon enter a time that brightens your life. There is positive news on the horizon. A situation you nurture blossoms. Following your heart brings excitement and adventure calls. It lets you make strides in developing a path that holds significant meaning. Your hopes and dreams are returned into your life when you connect with, blossoms into an approach you can grow. It brings a social theme that increases your sense of security. It has the potential to become a significant turning point for your life. As you mingle and network, you find your confidence is returning.

**5 Monday**

**6 Tuesday**

**7 Wednesday**

**8 Thursday** ~ Full Moon in Gemini 04:07
Cold Moon, Moon Before Yule
Mars at Opposition

**9 Friday**

**10 Saturday**

**11 Sunday**

Angel Jeremiel says that it is time for surprise reconnections. A person has been thinking about you and hopes to revisit a past chapter. Synchronicity is guiding the path ahead. It creates the right environment for this person to bridge the gap. When they first sync up with you, the conversation is light and casual. This person hopes to develop a closer bond with you. There is a chance to revisit the past and go over old ground with someone you haven't heard from recently. It brings open and honest communication that clears the air with this person. Reconnecting with this individual draws stability and security into your world. It has you feeling valued, and this creates a fantastic foundation. This person is hoping to check in with you soon.

**12 Monday**

**13 Tuesday** ~ Geminids Meteor Shower. December 7-17

**14 Wednesday**

**15 Thursday**

**16 Friday** ~ Last Quarter Moon in Virgo 08:56

**17 Saturday**

**18 Sunday** ~ Hanukkah (begins at sunset)

Angel Haniel shares that something is on offer, which gets things on track to be a spectacular time for your life. This new potential ignites and inspires your mind. It brings a chapter that marks a significant improvement occurring. Advancing and progressing your options is the ticket to a phase of improved good fortune. There is a sense of purpose and a feeling that your goals line up beautifully when this opportunity lands in your lap. As you shift your focus on achieving your vision, you discover innovative ways to overcome hurdles and sidestep barriers. Mapping out avenues of growth underscores your willingness to develop your life.

**19 Monday**

**20 Tuesday**

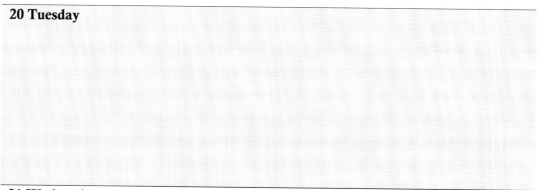

**21 Wednesday** ~ Mercury at Greatest Eastern elongation of 20.1 degrees from Sun
Ursids Meteor Shower December 17 – 25
Yule/Winter Solstice at 09:48

**22 Thursday**

**23 Friday** ~ New Moon in Capricorn 10:16

**24 Saturday**

**25 Sunday** ~ Christmas Day

Archangel Ariel says that a social aspect hits the ticket for drawing happiness into your life. You improve your circumstances by focusing on spending time with the people who elevate your potential. It does leave the drama at the door. Setting your intentions takes your hopes and dreams further. It brings a chance to mingle when life offers opportunities to spend time with kindred spirits. It kicks off a bountiful cycle for your social life. It brings brainstorming sessions with like-minded people, which adds an engaging sense of community to your world.

**26 Monday** ~ Boxing Day (Canada & UK)
Hanukkah (ends at sunset)
Christmas Day (observed)
Kwanzaa Begins

**27 Tuesday**

**28 Wednesday**

**29 Thursday** ~ Mercury Retrograde begins in Capricorn

**30 Friday** ~ First Quarter Moon Aries 01:21

**31 Saturday** ~ New Year's Eve

**1 Sunday** ~ New Year's Day
Kwanzaa ends

Angel Raguel says that changes arrive that create a growth-orientated phase. Setting your aspirations and develop a cohesive structure to your ideas to build a stable foundation for growth. The fires of your creativity and inspiration burn brightly and open a path that advances your vision. Opportunity is looming; it brings new horizons and fresh energy that rejuvenates your spirit. It helps you reach for a prestigious dream. Gaining insight about the path ahead lights the way towards your vision. Setting intentions and working with manifestation draws valuable results.

## About Crystal Sky

Crystal is passionate about the universe, helping others, and personal development. She writes yearly horoscopes diaries for each star sign. She produces a range of astrologically minded journals to celebrate the universal forces which affect us all. You can visit to learn more about Crystal's books and personal astrology readings by visiting the website.

www.psychic-emails.com

When not writing about the stars, you can find Crystal under them, gazing up at the abundance that surrounds us all, with her pup Henri by her side.

Printed in Great Britain
by Amazon

74860102R00116